Theory Paper   Grade 5   2019   A
Model Answers

1

(a) (i)   (3)

(ii)   **X**   submediant   (2)

     Y   subdominant   (2)

(b) (i)   Chord **A**   I   3rd / Ib   (2)

     Chord **B**   IV   5th / IVc   (2)

(ii)   (2)

(iii) acciaccatura / grace note / crushed note   (2)

2 (a)   augmented 3rd   perfect 5th   minor 6th   (6)

(b)   (4)

3   (10)

4 (a) (i)   *moderato*   (2)

(ii)   (4)

(iii) B minor   (2)

(iv)   (2)

or

or

(b) (i)   A   (2)

(ii)   (4)

(iii) true   (2)

       false   (2)

(c) (i)   compound   (2)

          duple

(ii)   *baritone*   (2)

(iii)   Instrument   violin / viola / cello / double bass   Family   strings   (4)

(iv) For violin / viola / cello: non-transposing

       For double bass: transposing   (2)

5 (a)   (10)

(b)

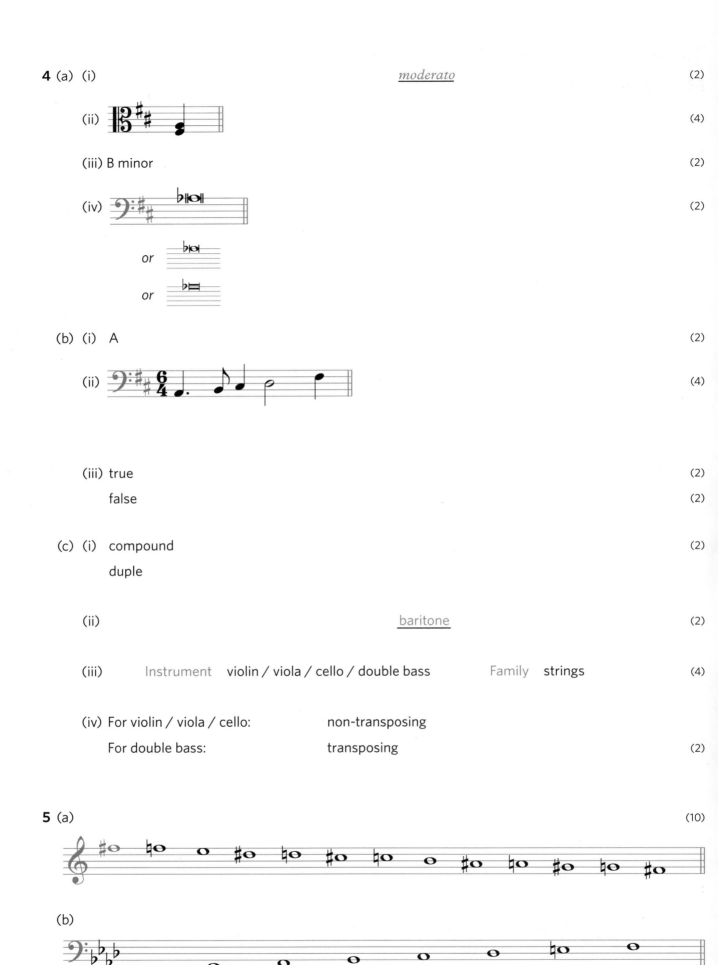

6 (a) (2)

(b) (6)

tenerezza means:		*ad lib.* means:		*estinto* means:	
tenderness	✔	in the style of	☐	as fast as possible	☐
heavy	☐	at choice	✔	expressive	☐
spirited	☐	in the same way	☐	calm	☐
sad, mournful	☐	becoming more lively	☐	as soft as possible	✔

(c)   demisemiquaver / 32nd note (2)

(d)   mordent / lower mordent (2)

(e) (3)

7 (10)

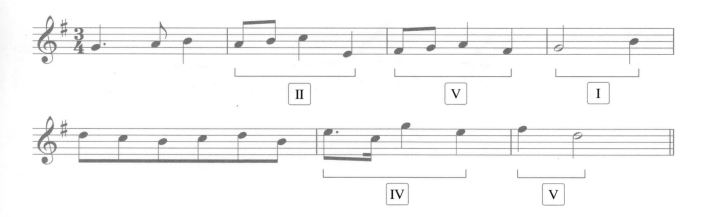

Theory Paper   Grade 5   2019   B
Model Answers

1

(a) (i)   (4)

(ii)   (2)

or

or

(iii) 24   (2)

(iv) F sharp   (2)

(b) (i)   (3)

etc.

(ii) mordent / lower mordent   (2)

2 (a)   perfect 4th   major 6th   minor 7th   (6)

(b)   (4)

3   (10)

4

(a) (i) **Adagio** means: ⦃ means: (4)

gradually getting slower	☐	spread the notes of the chord quickly, starting from the bottom	✔
at a medium speed	☐	glissando	☐
held back	☐	spread the notes of the chord quickly, starting from the top	☐
slow	✔	press the left pedal	☐

(ii)   D minor   (2)

(iii) *Both possible answers are shown on the extract reproduced below. For full marks candidates need to identify*
       only one example of the answer.   (2)

(iv)   turn / upper turn   (2)

(b) (i)   (4)

(ii)   Chord **A** (bar 3)   IV root / IVa   (2)

       Chord **B** (bar 3)   I 5th / Ic   (2)

       Chord **C** (bar 3)   V root / Va   (2)

(c) (i)   false   (2)

(ii)   simple   (2)

       quadruple

(iii)   Instrument   violin / viola / harp   Family   strings   (4)

       or   Instrument   flute / oboe / clarinet   Family   woodwind

       or   Instrument   trumpet   Family   brass

       or   Instrument   xylophone / vibraphone / celesta /   Family   percussion
                           marimba

(iv)   Non-transposing :   violin / viola / harp / flute / oboe / vibraphone / marimba   (2)
              Transposing :   clarinet / trumpet / xylophone / celesta

5 (10)

(a)

(b)

6 (a) *sonoro* means: (2)

in an undertone ☐

dying away ☐

resonant, with a rich tone ✔

singing ☐

(b) two / two quavers / two eighth notes / one crotchet / one quarter note / one beat (2)

(c) **X** (bar 1)   supertonic (2)

Y (bar 3)   submediant (2)

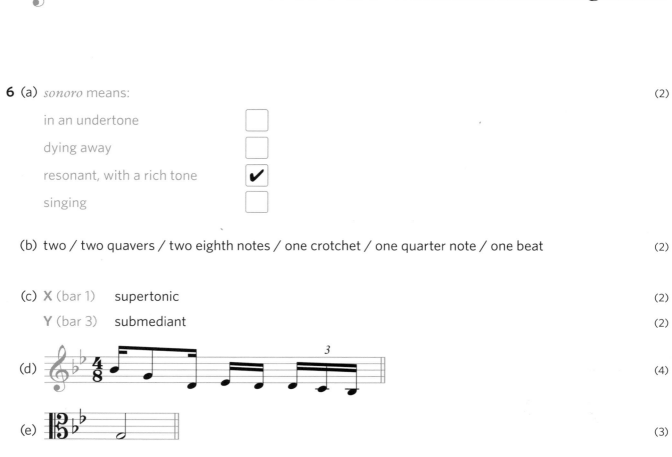

(d) (4)

(e) (3)

7 (10)

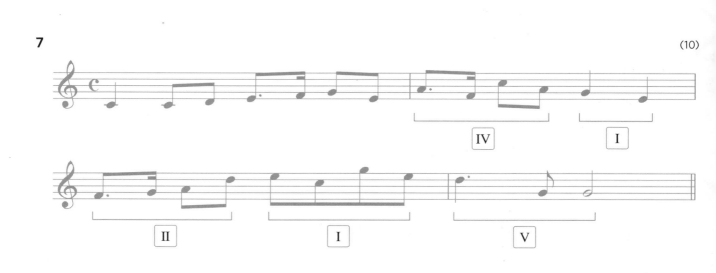

Theory Paper Grade 5 2019 C
Model Answers

1 (a) (i)   Chord **A** (bar 3)   IV root / IVa   (2)

Chord **B** (bar 3)   I 3rd / Ib   (2)

(ii)   (2)

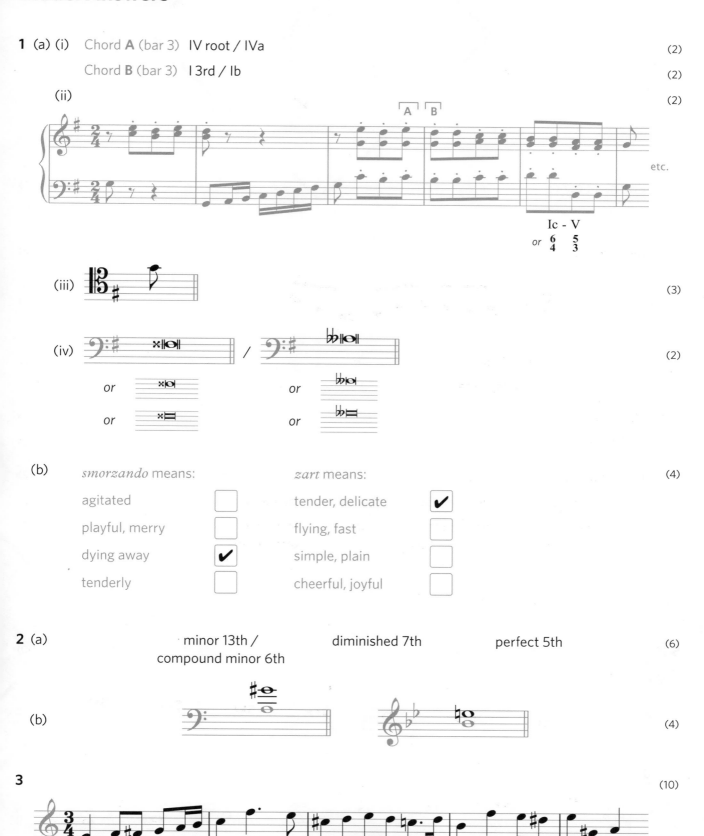

etc.

Ic - V

or $\begin{smallmatrix}6\\4\end{smallmatrix}$ $\begin{smallmatrix}5\\3\end{smallmatrix}$

(iii)   (3)

(iv)   (2)

or   or

or   or

(b)   *smorzando* means: *zart* means: (4)

agitated   ☐   tender, delicate   ✔

playful, merry   ☐   flying, fast   ☐

dying away   ✔   simple, plain   ☐

tenderly   ☐   cheerful, joyful   ☐

2 (a)   minor 13th /   diminished 7th   perfect 5th   (6)
compound minor 6th

(b)   (4)

3   (10)

4 (a) (i)   (6)

non troppo means: **lento** means: *cantabile* means:

very much   ☐   very slow   ☐   in a singing style   ☑

not too much   ☑   gradually getting ☐   smoothly   ☐
                              slower

not in time   ☐   slow   ☑   gradually getting   ☐
                                                            quieter

too much   ☐   held back   ☐   repeat from the   ☐
                                                            beginning

    (ii)   compound   (2)

           triple

    (iii) A♭ major   (2)

(b) (i)   (6)

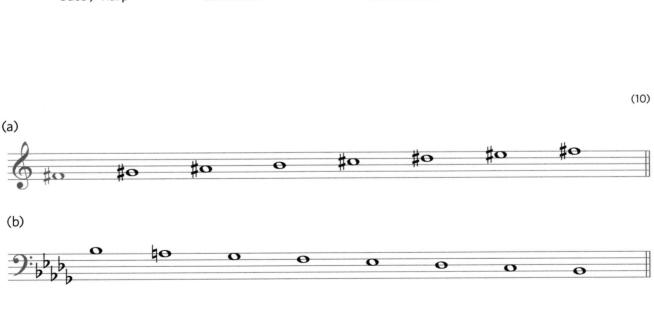

    (ii) **X** (bar 6)   mediant   (2)

            Y (bar 8)   leading note   (2)

(c) (i)   true   (2)

           false   (2)

    (ii) woodwind   (2)

         strings   or   brass   or   percussion   (2)

         double bass /   or   tuba /   or   timpani /   (2)
         bass / harp   bass tuba   kettledrums

5   (10)

  (a)

  (b)

6

(a) (2)

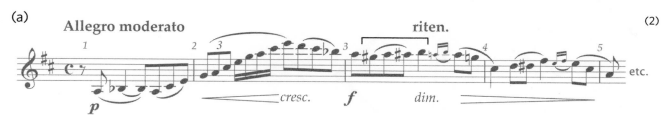

(b) 12 (2)

(c) (4)

(d) D (2)

two / two quavers / two eighth notes / one crotchet / one quarter note / one beat (2)

(e) grace notes (2)

(f) E / E natural (1)

7 (10)

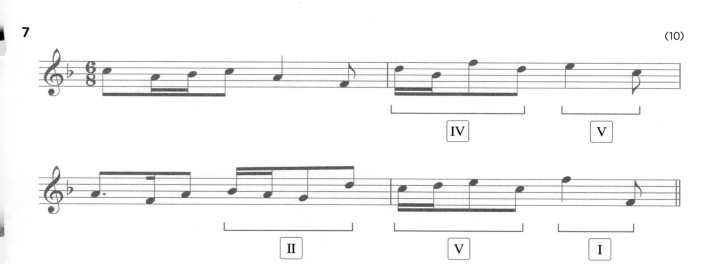

Theory Paper   Grade 5   2019   S
Model Answers

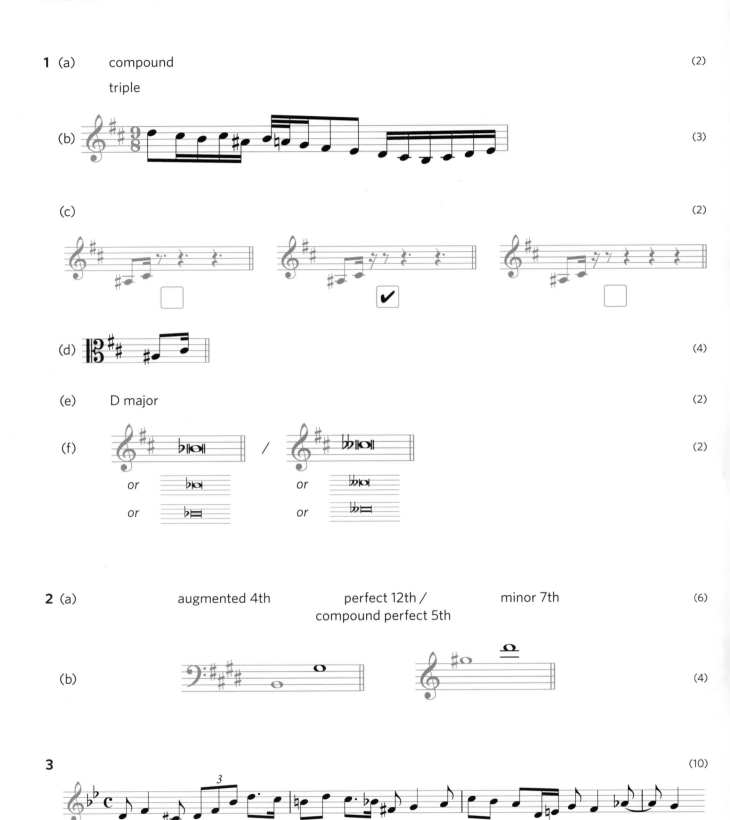

1 (a)   compound   (2)

   triple

   (b)   (3)

   (c)   (2)

   (d)   (4)

   (e)   D major   (2)

   (f)   (2)

   or   *or*

   or   *or*

2 (a)   augmented 4th   perfect 12th /   minor 7th   (6)
                                        compound perfect 5th

   (b)   (4)

3   (10)

4

(a) (i)

⊓ means:		**ritenuto** means:		(4)
down bow	✔	gradually getting quicker	☐	
up bow	☐	slow	☐	
pluck the string with the finger	☐	held back	✔	
with mute	☐	gradually getting slower	☐	

(ii) *süss* (2)

(iii) (4)

(b) (i) A minor (2)

(ii) Chord **A** (bar 3)   IV root / IVa (2)

  Chord **B** (bar 3)   I 3rd / Ib (2)

(iii) (4)

(c) (i) twelve (2)

(ii)

Family	woodwind	Instrument	bassoon / double bassoon	(4)
or Family	brass	Instrument	tuba / bass tuba	
or Family	percussion	Instrument	timpani / kettledrums	

(iii) false (2)

   true (2)

5 (10)

(a)

(b)

6 (a) **A**   turn / upper turn / grupetto (2)

   B   appoggiatura / grace note (2)

(b)  (5)

(c) (2)

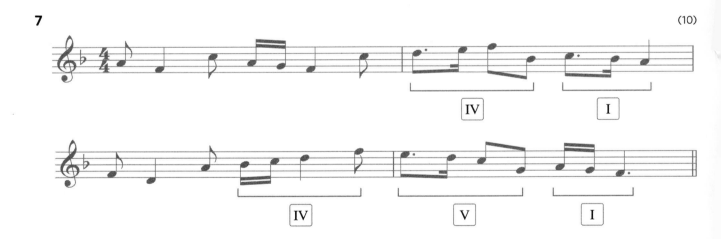

(d)   **X**   leading note (2)

   Y   subdominant (2)

7 (10)

Music Theory Practice Papers 2019 Model Answers

Model answers for four practice papers from ABRSM's 2019 Theory exams for Grade 5

Key features:

- a list of correct answers where appropriate
- a selection of likely options where the answer can be expressed in a variety of ways
- a single exemplar where a composition-style answer is required

Support material for ABRSM Music Theory exams

**Supporting the teaching and learning of music
in partnership with four Royal Schools of Music**

Royal Academy of Music | Royal College of Music
Royal Northern College of Music | Royal Conservatoire of Scotland

www.abrsm.org f facebook.com/abrsm
🐦 @abrsm ▶ ABRSM YouTube

ISBN 978-1-78601-377-4

9 781786 013774

First Steps to Using Money

Book 3

Moira Wilson

Editor: Hayley Willer
Illustrations: Moira Wilson

Layout artist: Suzanne Ward
Cover design: Design for Marketing, Ware

© 1996 Folens Limited, on behalf of the author.

Every effort has been made to contact copyright holders of material used in this book. If any have been overlooked, we will be pleased to make any necessary arrangements.

British Library Cataloguing in Publication Data. A catalogue record for this book is available from the British Library.

First published 1996 by Folens Limited, Dunstable and Dublin.
Folens Limited, Albert House, Apex Business Centre, Boscombe Road, Dunstable, LU5 4RL, England.

ISBN 1 85276946–7

Printed in Singapore by Craft Print.

Contents

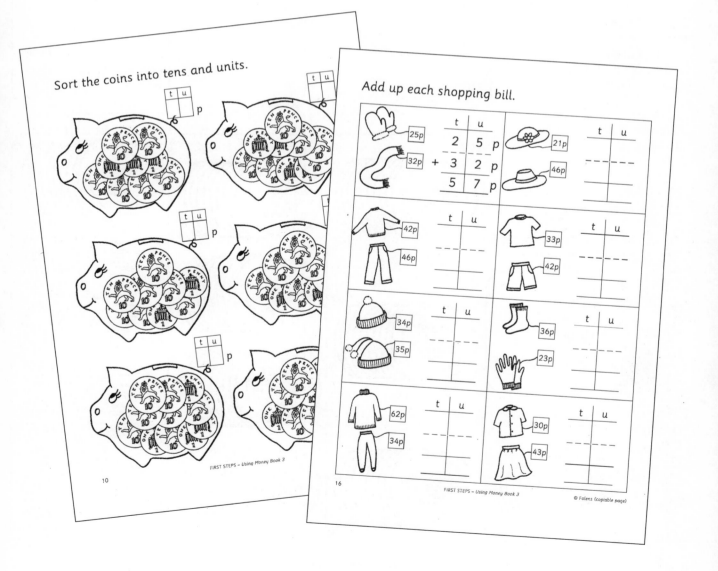

Exchange the piles of penny coins for 10p coins.

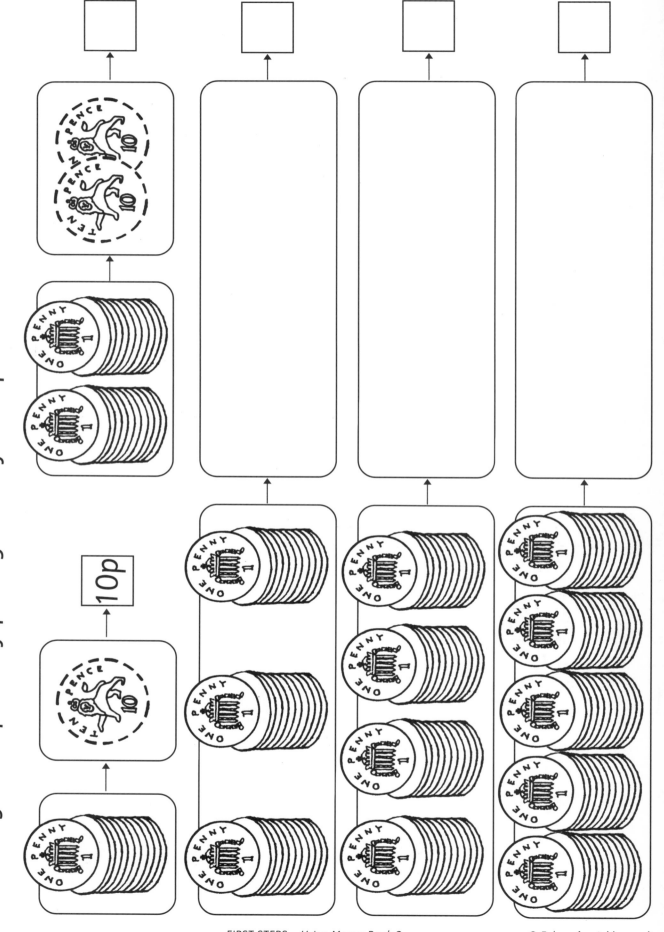

FIRST STEPS – *Using Money Book 3* © Folens (copiable page)

Work out the number of 10p coins hidden in each jar.

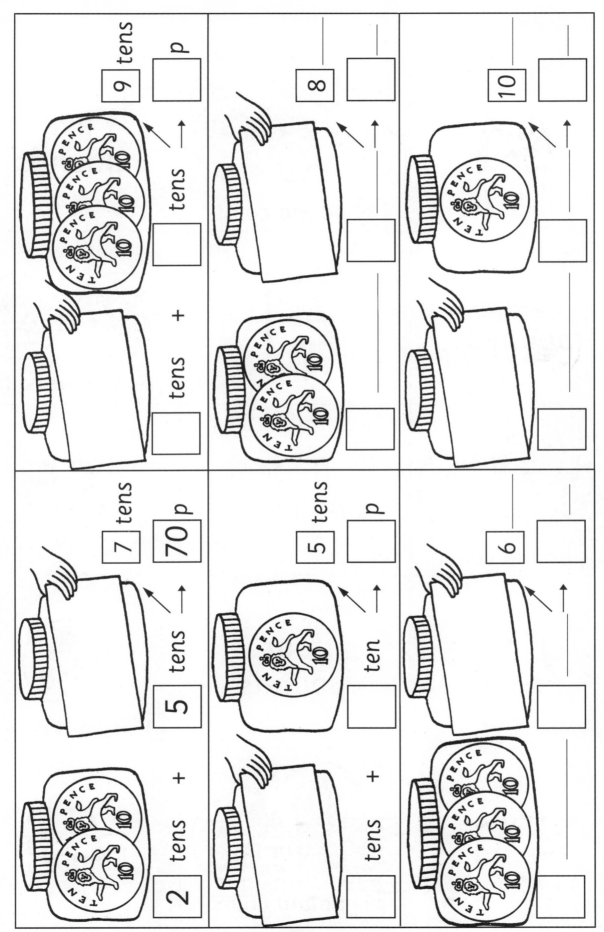

| 9 | tens |
| | p |

| 7 | tens |
| 70 | p |

| 8 | ___ |
| | p |

| 5 | tens |
| | p |

| 10 | ___ |
| | ___ |

| 6 | ___ |
| | ___ |

Make up your own hidden coin sums and test a friend.

Sort into groups.

£4	 3 pound coins	five pounds
two pounds	£1	 2 pound coins
 4 pound coins	three pounds	£5
£2	four pounds	 1 pound coin
one pound	 5 pound coins	£3

Put a 10p coin in each hand.

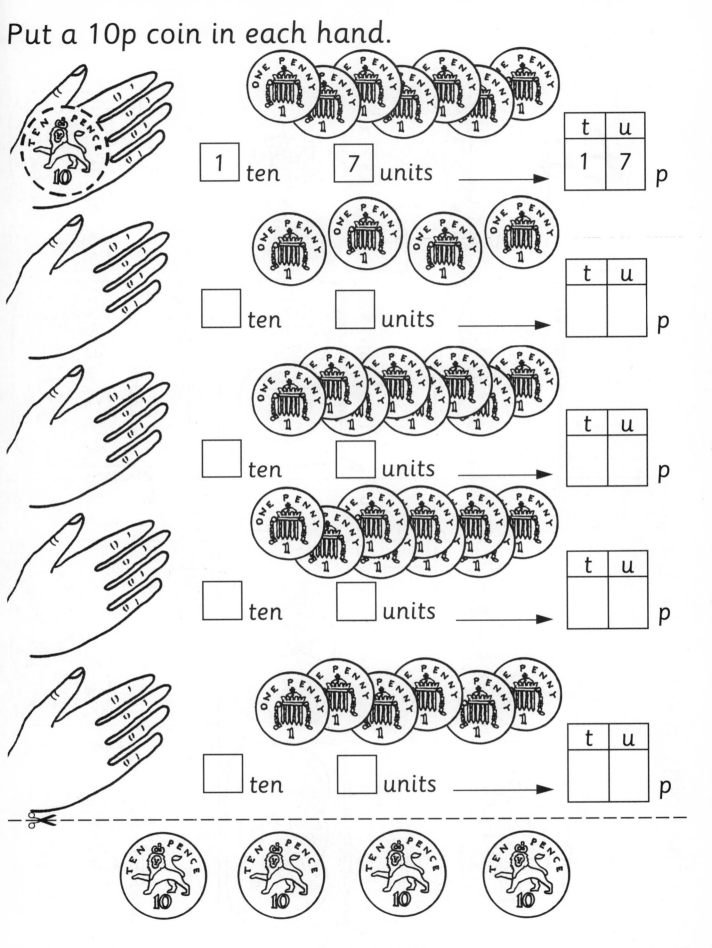

t	u
1	7

1 ten   7 units → $\boxed{17}$ p

ten   units → p

ten   units → p

ten   units → p

ten   units → p

Sort the coins into tens and units.

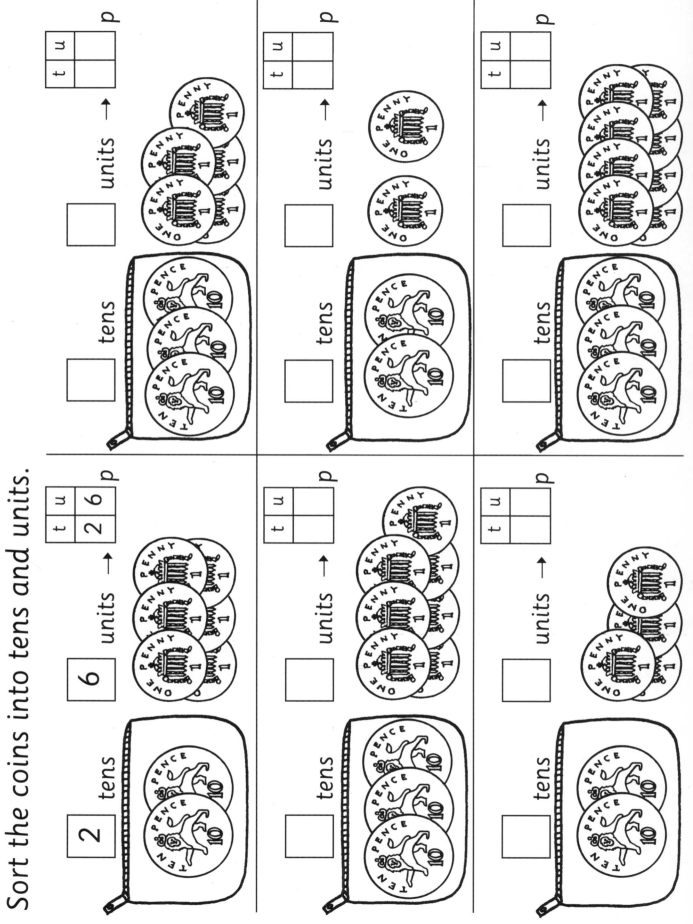

Sort the coins into tens and units.

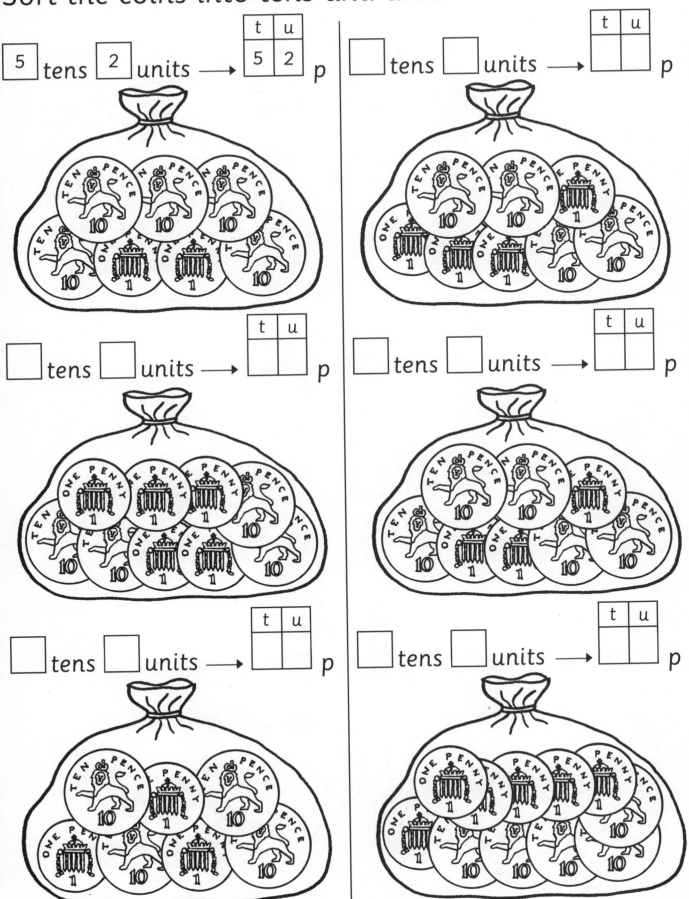

[5] tens [2] units → | t | u |
                     |---|---|
                     | 5 | 2 | p

[ ] tens [ ] units → | t | u |
                     |---|---|
                     | | | p

[ ] tens [ ] units → | t | u |
                     |---|---|
                     | | | p

[ ] tens [ ] units → | t | u |
                     |---|---|
                     | | | p

[ ] tens [ ] units → | t | u |
                     |---|---|
                     | | | p

[ ] tens [ ] units → | t | u |
                     |---|---|
                     | | | p

Sort the coins into tens and units.

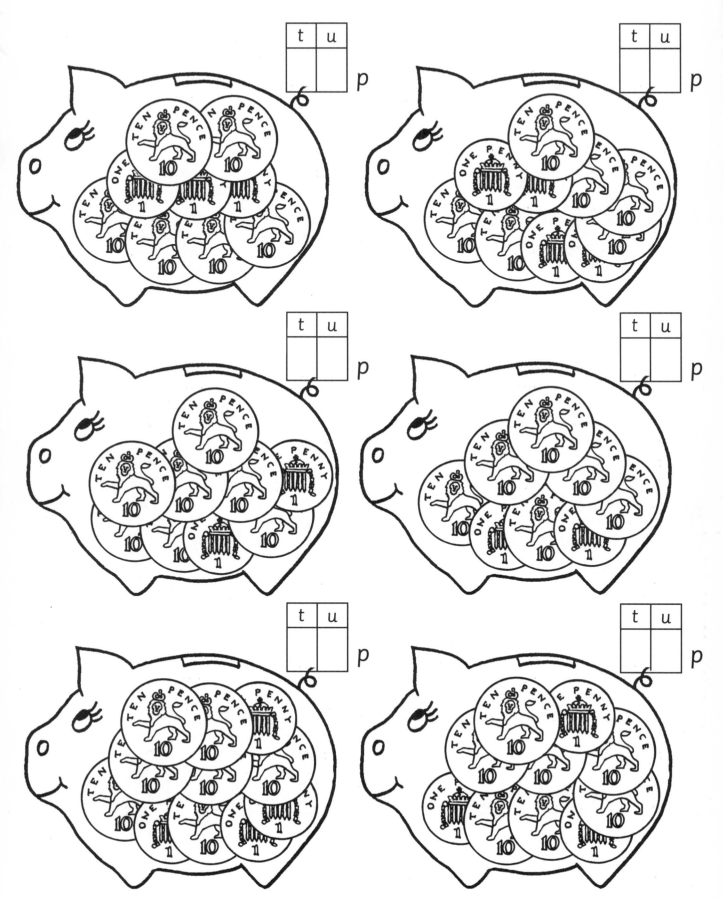

FIRST STEPS – *Using Money Book 3*

© Folens (copiable page)

Sort the coins into tens and units.

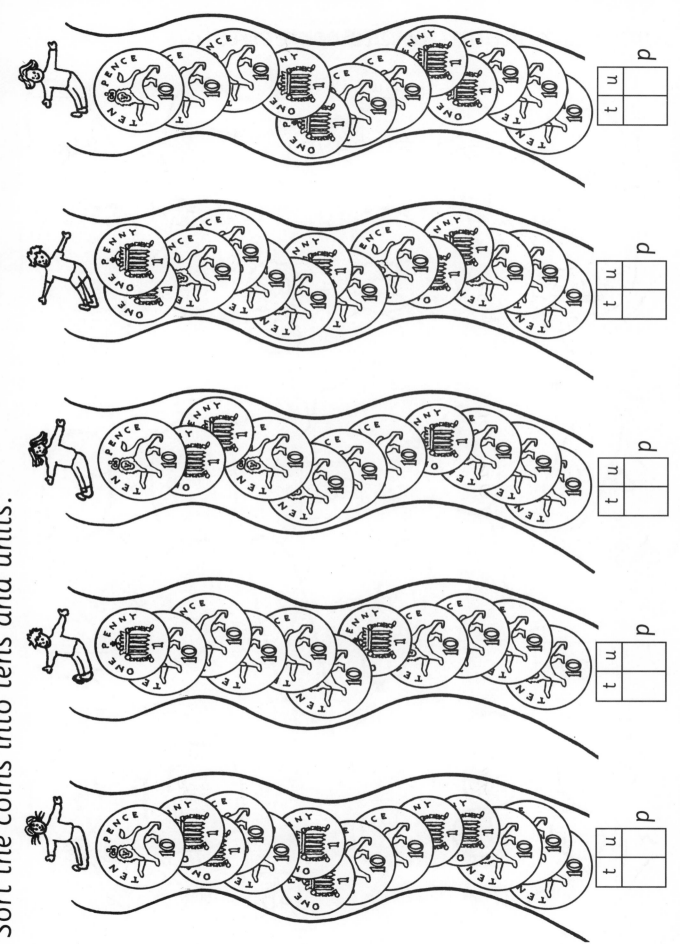

Join the balloons to the correct totals.

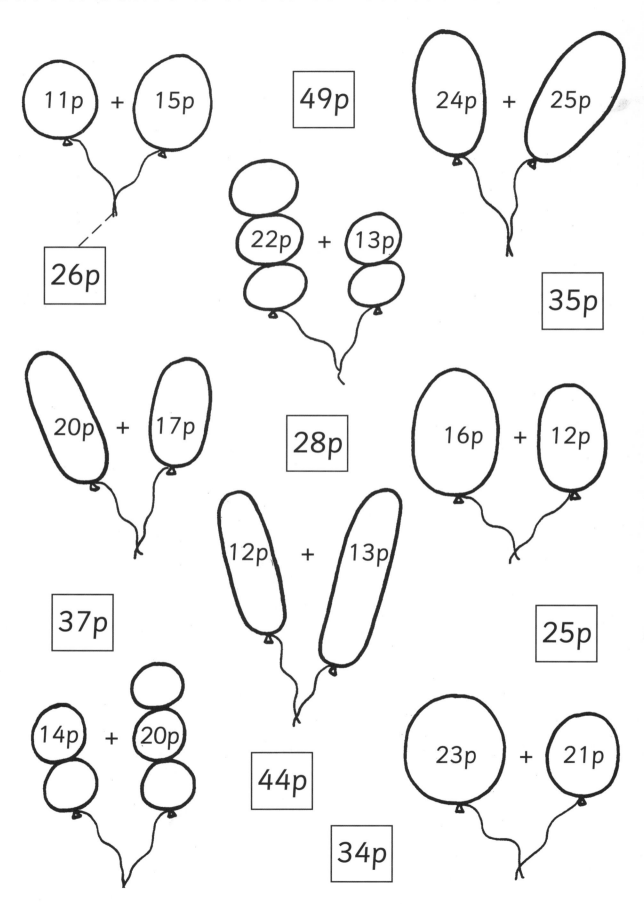

11p + 15p

49p

24p + 25p

26p

22p + 13p

35p

20p + 17p

28p

16p + 12p

37p

12p + 13p

25p

14p + 20p

44p

23p + 21p

34p

FIRST STEPS – Using Money Book 3

Add up each shopping bill.

16p
13p

t	u	
1	6	p
+ 1	3	p
2	9	p

24p
23p

t	u

12p
15p

t	u

25p
11p

t	u

22p
23p

t	u

18p
31p

t	u

17p
21p

t	u

20p
19p

t	u

Add up each shopping bill.

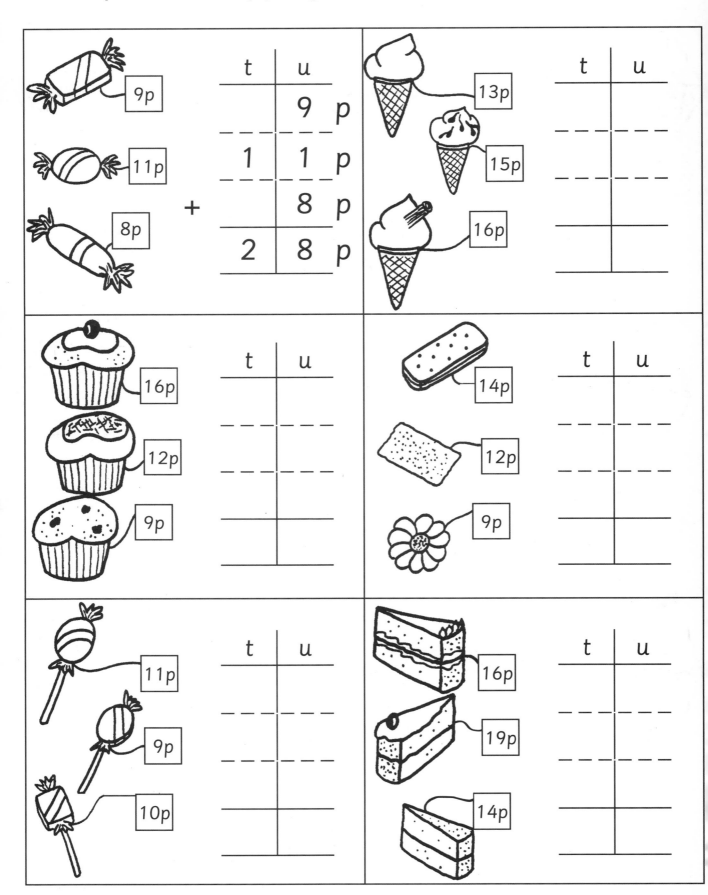

Box 1 (candy/sweets):
- 9p
- 11p
- 8p

	t	u	
		9	p
+	1	1	p
		8	p
	2	8	p

Box 2 (ice creams):
- 13p
- 15p
- 16p

t	u

Box 3 (cupcakes):
- 16p
- 12p
- 9p

t	u

Box 4 (biscuits/flower):
- 14p
- 12p
- 9p

t	u

Box 5 (lollipops):
- 11p
- 9p
- 10p

t	u

Box 6 (cake slices):
- 16p
- 19p
- 14p

t	u

Join the kites to the correct totals.

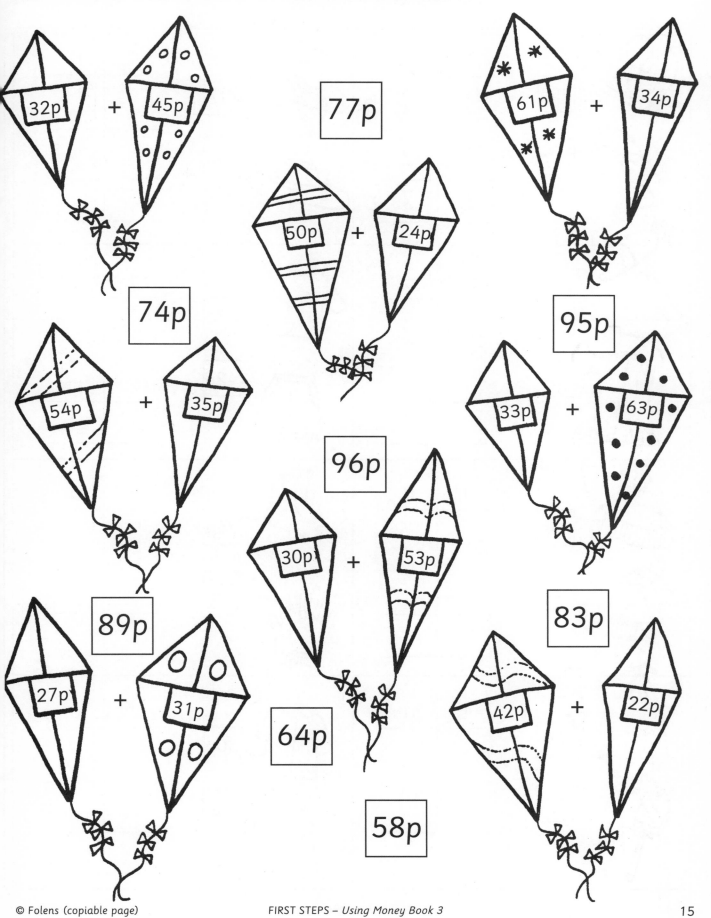

32p + 45p

77p

61p + 34p

50p + 24p

74p

95p

54p + 35p

33p + 63p

96p

30p + 53p

83p

27p + 31p

89p

64p

42p + 22p

58p

Add up each shopping bill.

	t	u	
	2	5	p
+	3	2	p
	5	7	p

25p
32p

t	u

21p
46p

t	u

42p
46p

t	u

33p
42p

t	u

34p
35p

t	u

36p
23p

t	u

62p
34p

t	u

30p
43p

Add up each shopping bill.

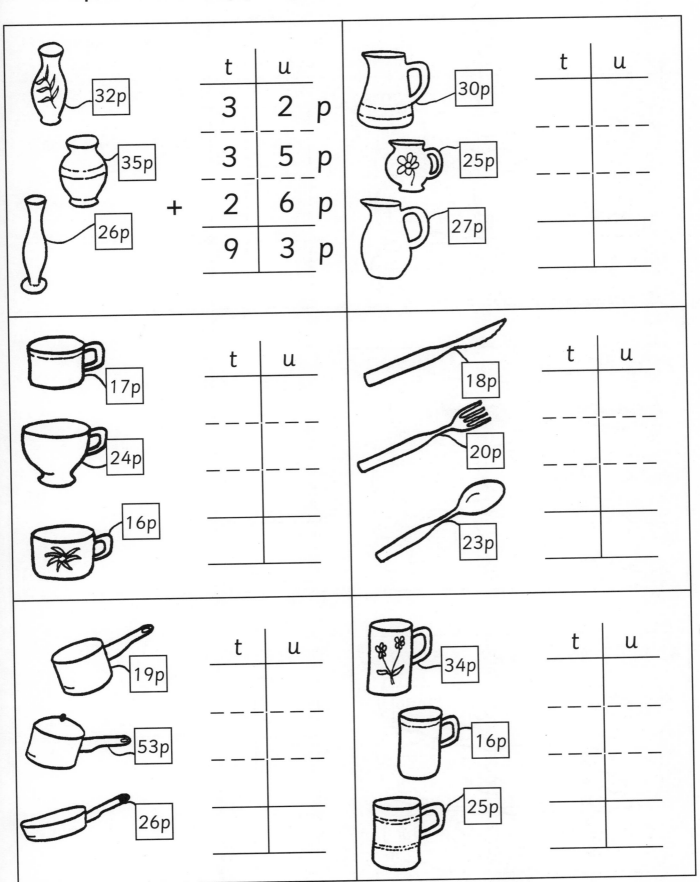

	t	u	
	3	2	p
	3	5	p
+	2	6	p
	9	3	p

Count on to find the difference in price.

$\overset{1\quad 2\quad 3\quad 4\quad 5\quad 6}{\curvearrowright\curvearrowright\curvearrowright\curvearrowright\curvearrowright\curvearrowright}$	The difference in price is	We can write it like this
21 22 23 24 25 26 27 28 29 30 31 24p ~~~ 30p 23p ~~~ 27p 21p ~~~ 26p	**6p** ☐ ☐	30p – 24p = 6p _____ _____
32 33 34 35 36 37 38 39 40 41 42 33p ~~~ 40p 35p ~~~ 37p 38p ~~~ 41p	☐ ☐ ☐	_____ _____ _____
43 44 45 46 47 48 49 50 51 52 53 43p ~~~ 48p 44p ~~~ 50p 46p ~~~ 49p	☐ ☐ ☐	_____ _____ _____

FIRST STEPS – *Using Money Book 3*   © Folens (copiable page)

Count on to find the difference in price.

1 2 3 4 5	The difference in price is	We can write it like this
63 64 65 66 67 68 69 70 71 72 73 🐱 cup 64p plate 69p fork 65p knife 72p spoon 66p spoon 68p	5p	69p – 64p = 5p
74 75 76 77 78 79 80 81 82 83 84 cup 76p mug 82p jug 74p jug 84p bowl 75p bowl 83p		
85 86 87 88 89 90 91 92 93 94 95 glass 88p glass 91p vase 89p vase 93p pan 86p pan 95p		

FIRST STEPS – Using Money Book 3   19

Use the coins to work out your change.

Exchange [50 FIFTY PENCE] for 4 [10 TEN PENCE] coins
10 [1 ONE PENNY] coins

Buy	Change from 50p	Buy	Change from 50p
cupcake 29p	21p	ice cream 31p	
sweet 8p		cake 45p	
ice cream 32p		sweet 6p	
sweet 13p		cupcake 24p	
cake 44p		sweet 17p	

FIRST STEPS – Using Money Book 3

© Folens (copiable page)

Use the coins to work out your change.

Exchange for 9 coins

10 coins

Buy	Change from £1	Buy	Change from £1
86p	14p	98p	
14p		62p	
37p		25p	
56p		73p	
9p		41p	

Give Jacob his change using as few coins as possible.

Jacob buys	He pays with	His change is
🖌 17p	20	2 1
😀 45p	50	
🐥 9p	20	
🧸 38p	50	
📏 16p	20	
🖊 14p	20	
📖 Birds 29p	50	

Give Sara her change using as few coins as possible.

Sara buys	She pays with	Her change is
46p	50 FIFTY PENCE	TWO PENCE 2 TWO PENCE 2
47p	ONE POUND	
58p	ONE POUND	
35p	50 FIFTY PENCE	
92p	ONE POUND	
28p	50 FIFTY PENCE	
19p	50 FIFTY PENCE	

FIRST STEPS – *Using Money Book 3*

Give James his change using as few coins as possible.

James buys	He pays with	His change is
Animals 42p	50 FIFTY PENCE	5 FIVE PENCE 2 TWO PENCE 1 ONE PENNY
44p	ONE POUND	
91p	ONE POUND	
7p	50 FIFTY PENCE	
68p	ONE POUND	
36p	50 FIFTY PENCE	
25p	50 FIFTY PENCE	

FIRST STEPS – Using Money Book 3

Draw 50p in each purse.
Use these coins.

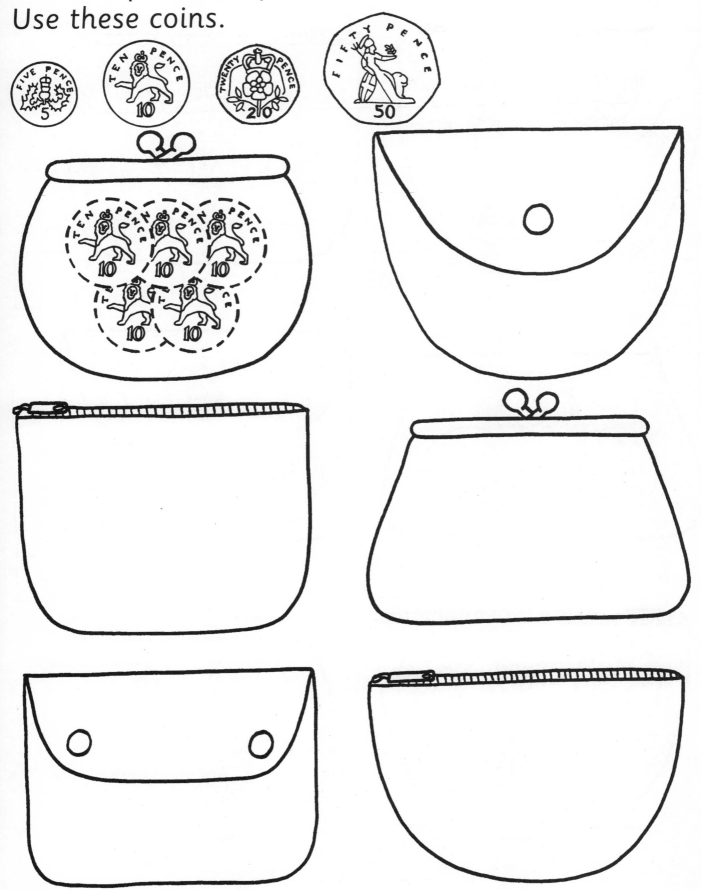

How much money is in each purse?

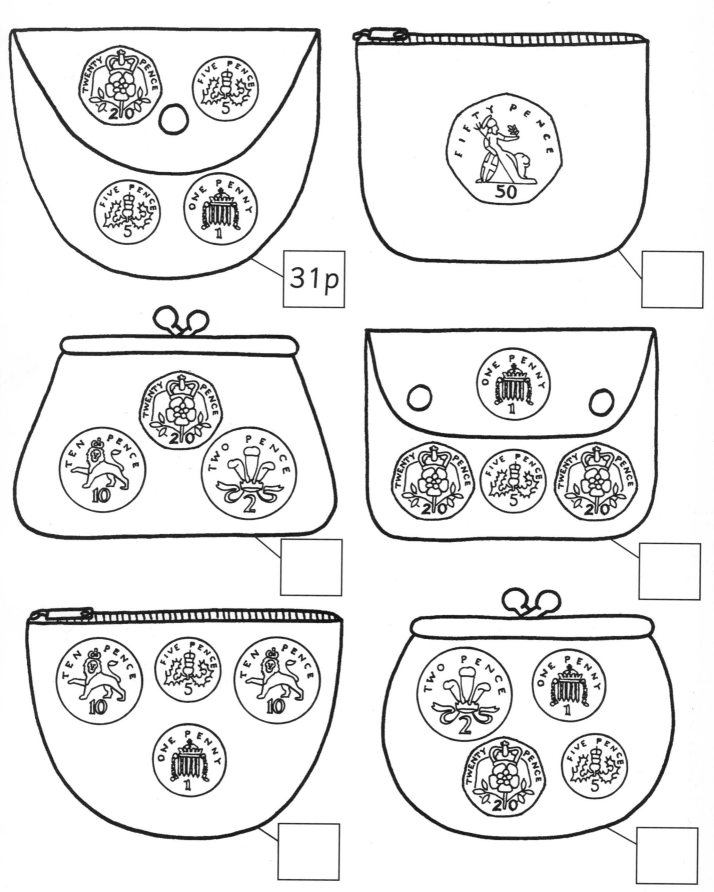

31p

FIRST STEPS – *Using Money Book 3*   © Folens (copiable page)

Draw £1 in each money bank.

Use these coins.

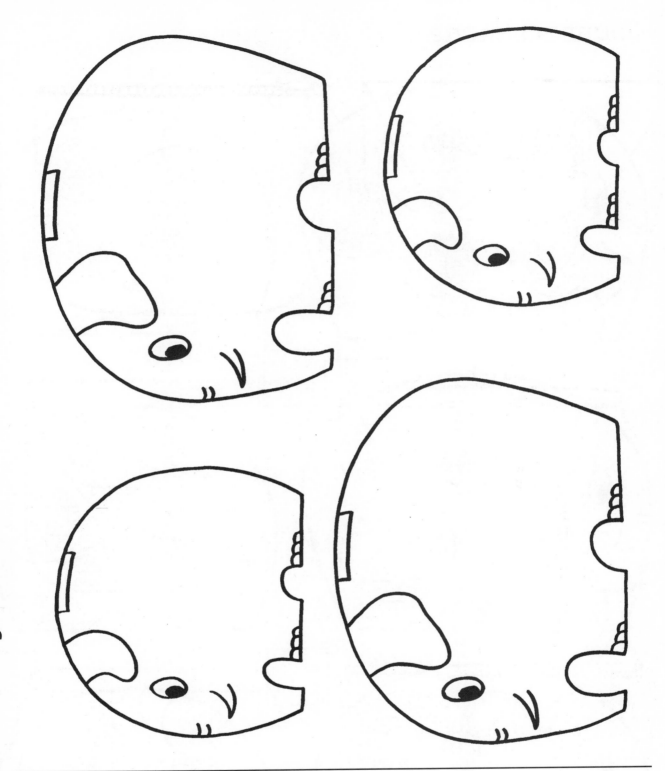

FIRST STEPS – *Using Money Book 3*

Count the money.

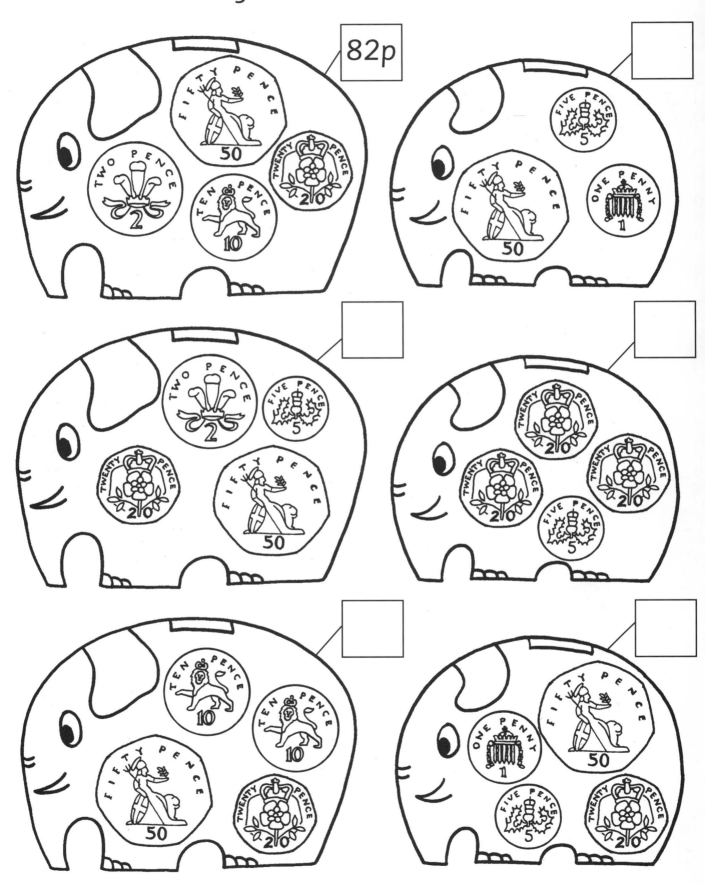

82p

FIRST STEPS – *Using Money Book 3*

© Folens (copiable page)

Sort into groups.

£3.20		two pounds six pence
four pounds ten pence	£1.55	
	three pounds twenty pence	£1.24
£2.06	one pound fifty-five pence	
one pound twenty-four pence		£4.10

How much money is in each jar?

£2.55
_____

_____

_____

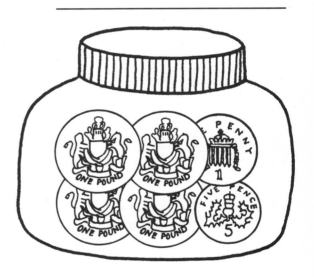

_____

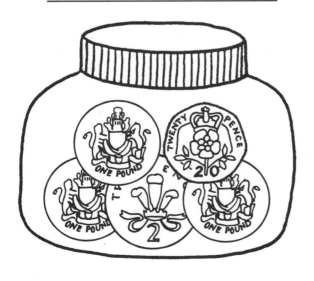

_____

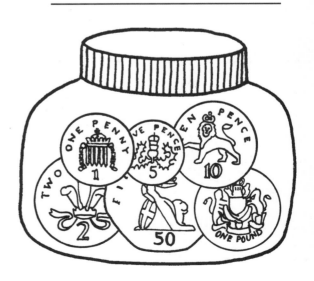

_____

FIRST STEPS – *Using Money Book 3*

Making patterns with 2p.

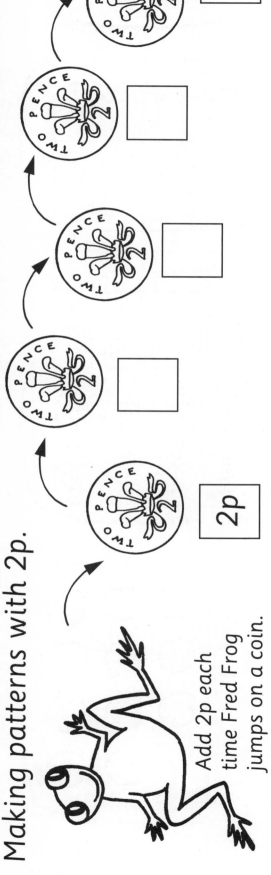

Add 2p each time Fred Frog jumps on a coin.

Continue this pattern.

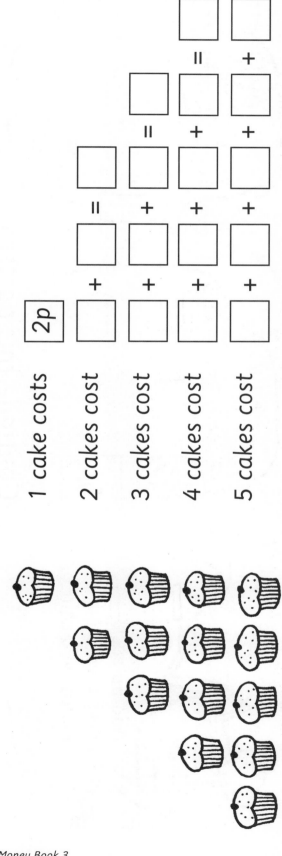

1 cake costs [2p]

2 cakes cost

3 cakes cost

4 cakes cost

5 cakes cost

FIRST STEPS – *Using Money Book 3*   31

Making patterns with 5p.

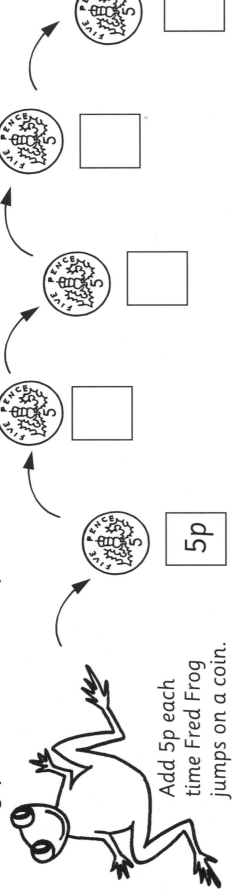

Add 5p each time Fred Frog jumps on a coin.

Continue this pattern.

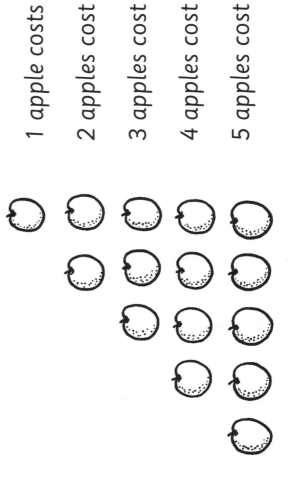

1 apple costs	5p			
2 apples cost	□	+	□	= □
3 apples cost	□	+	□	+ □ = □
4 apples cost	□	+	□	+ □ + □ = □
5 apples cost	□	+	□	+ □ + □ + □ = □

Making patterns with 10p.

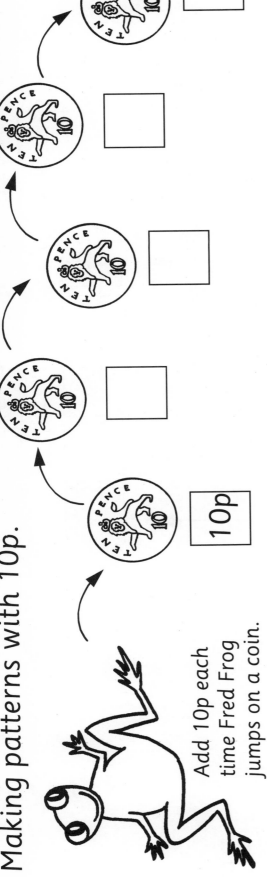

Add 10p each time Fred Frog jumps on a coin.

Continue this pattern.

1 pear costs	10p
2 pears cost	
3 pears cost	
4 pears cost	
5 pears cost	

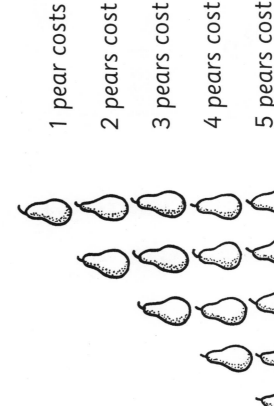

How much money is in each piggy bank?

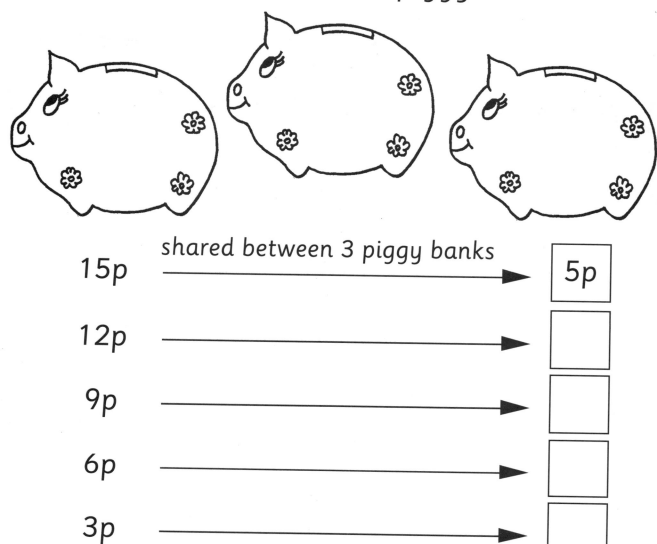

15p   shared between 3 piggy banks   → 5p

12p   →

9p   →

6p   →

3p   →

Can you continue this pattern?

15p – 3p = 12p

12p – 3p =

_____

_____

_____

FIRST STEPS – *Using Money Book 3*

How much money is in each purse?

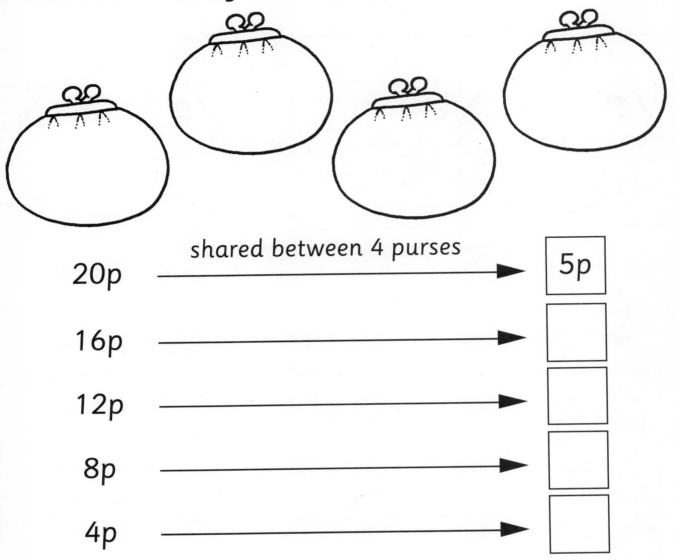

20p ——— shared between 4 purses ———▶ 5p

16p ————————————————————▶ ☐

12p ————————————————————▶ ☐

8p ————————————————————▶ ☐

4p ————————————————————▶ ☐

Can you continue this pattern?

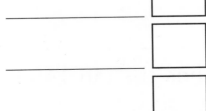

20p – 4p = 16p

16p – 4p = ☐

_____ ☐

_____ ☐

_____ ☐

Pay for each balloon with 2p coins.

I buy	I pay with
balloon **2p**	○ TWO PENCE 2
balloon **8p**	
balloon **4p**	
balloon **10p**	
balloon **6p**	

Draw your own balloons costing 14p, 12p, 18p, 16p and 20p. Pay with 2p coins.

FIRST STEPS – *Using Money Book 3*   © Folens (copiable page)

Pay for each pet with 5p coins.

I buy	I pay with
5p	
20p	
10p	
15p	
25p	

Draw your own pets costing 35p, 40p, 30p, 45p and 50p.
Pay with 5p coins.

Pay for each teddy with 10p coins.

I buy	I pay with
10p	
30p	
40p	
20p	
50p	

Draw your own teddies costing 70p, 90p, 60p, 80p and £1.
Pay with 10p coins.

FIRST STEPS – *Using Money Book 3*   © Folens (copiable page)

Work out the cost of the vegetables.

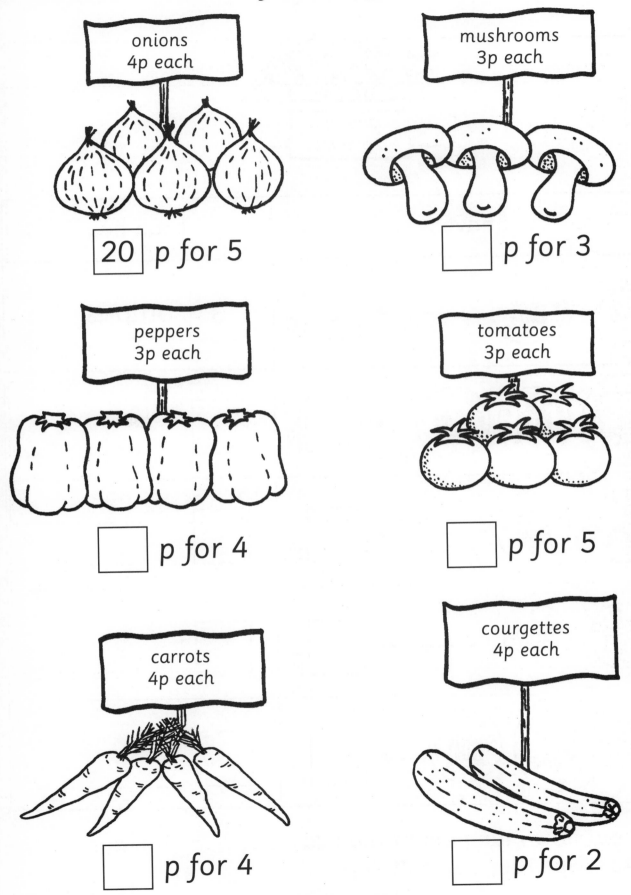

onions
4p each

20 p for 5

mushrooms
3p each

☐ p for 3

peppers
3p each

☐ p for 4

tomatoes
3p each

☐ p for 5

carrots
4p each

☐ p for 4

courgettes
4p each

☐ p for 2

How many onions can you buy?

onions
2p each

I have	I can buy
 (5p, 1p) → 6 p	3 onions
(2p, 1p, 1p) → ☐ p	☐ _____
(1p, 1p) → ☐ p	☐ _____
(5p, 5p) → ☐ p	☐ _____
(5p, 2p, 1p) → ☐ p	☐ _____

Work out how many onions you can buy
for 14p, 18p, 12p, 16p and 20p.

FIRST STEPS – *Using Money Book 3*   © Folens (copiable page)

How many oranges can you buy?

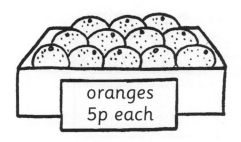

oranges
5p each

I have	I can buy
🪙10 🪙5 🪙5 → **20** p	**4** oranges
🪙5 🪙5 → ☐ p	☐ _____
🪙2 🪙2 🪙1 → ☐ p	☐ _____
🪙20 🪙5 → ☐ p	☐ _____
🪙5 🪙10 → ☐ p	☐ _____

Now work out how many oranges you can buy
for 35p, 45p, 30p, 40p and 50p.

How many apples can you buy?

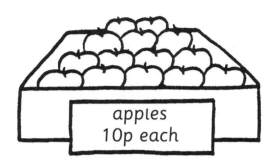

apples
10p each

I have		I can buy
10 5 5 → 20 p		2 apples
20 20 → ☐ p		☐ _____
50 → ☐ p		☐ _____
5 5 → ☐ p		☐ _____
20 10 → ☐ p		☐ _____

Work out how many apples you can buy
for 80p, 60p, 90p, 70p and £1.

FIRST STEPS – *Using Money Book 3*   © Folens (copiable page)

How much is each piece of fruit?

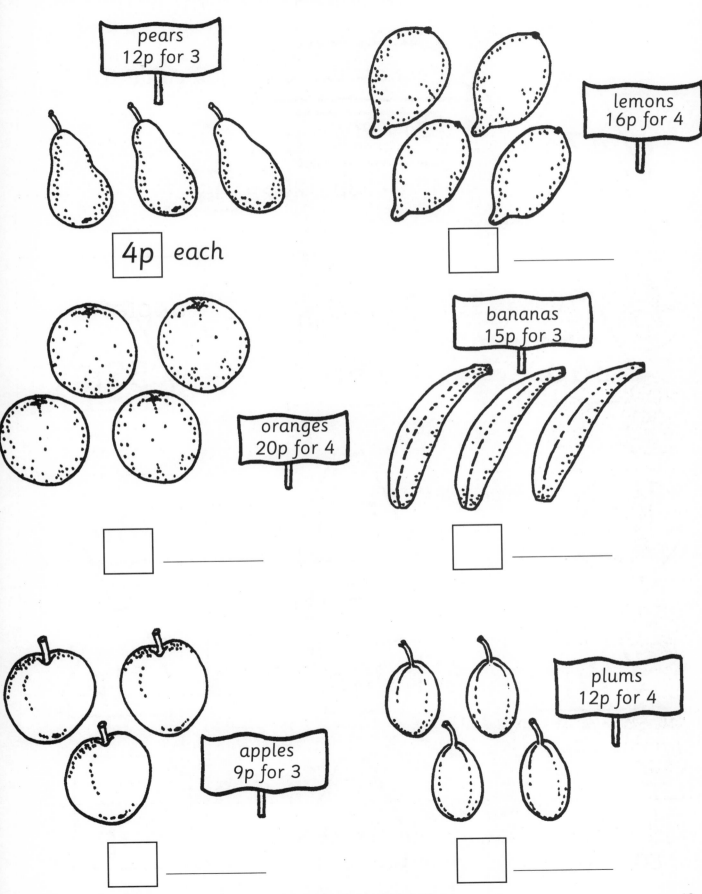

pears
12p for 3

4p each

lemons
16p for 4

oranges
20p for 4

bananas
15p for 3

apples
9p for 3

plums
12p for 4

FIRST STEPS – *Using Money Book 3*

Use a to find the missing money.

Here are two ways you could try.

23p + 20p + $\boxed{4p}$ = 47p

47p − 23p − 20p = $\boxed{4p}$

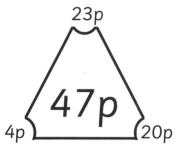

Now try these.

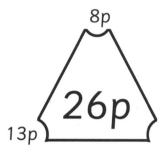

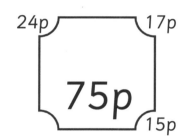

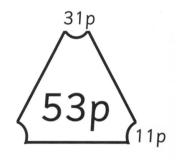

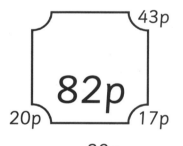

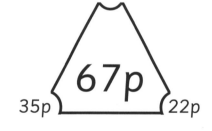

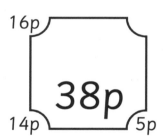

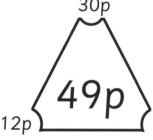

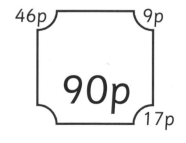

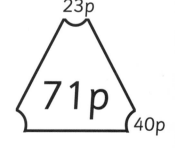

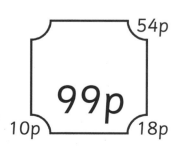

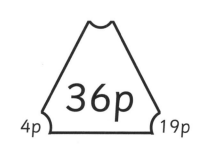

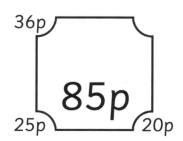

FIRST STEPS – *Using Money Book 3*

The rabbit game

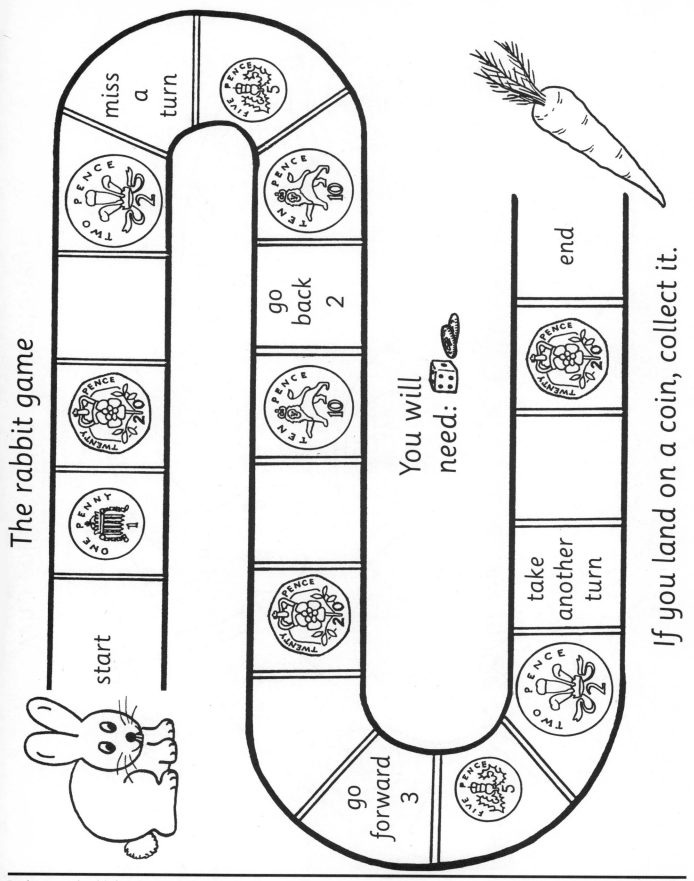

start

miss a turn

go back 2

go forward 3

You will need:

take another turn

end

If you land on a coin, collect it.

Teachers' notes (mask before photocopying)
Two players.
Equipment: a dice, two counters and real coins up to 20p.
The children take it in turns to throw the dice, moving along the correct number of spaces. If they land on a picture of a coin, they have to collect it.
When both children have reached the end, they count the money they have collected. The child with the most money is the winner.

The snake game

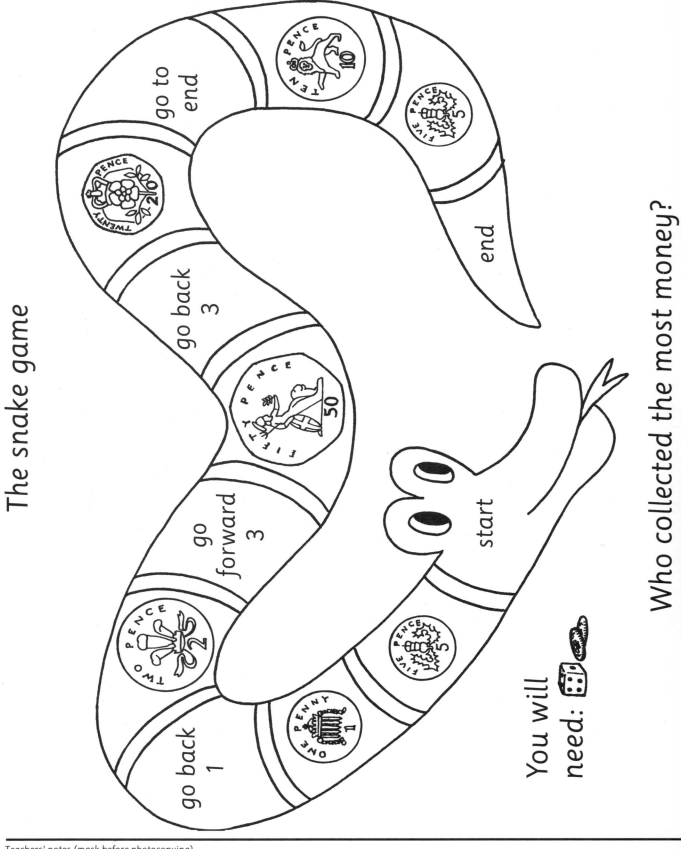

Who collected the most money?

Teachers' notes (mask before photocopying)
Two players.
Equipment: a dice, two counters and real coins up to 50p.
The children take it in turns to throw the dice, moving along the correct number of spaces. If they land on a picture of a coin, they have to collect it.
When both children have reached the end, they count the money they have collected. The child with the most money is the winner.

46   FIRST STEPS – *Using Money Book 3*   © Folens (copiable page)

Find the pairs game

54p		
	Joker Try again!	**80p**
23p		
41p	**60p**	**75p**
	32p	

Teachers' notes (mask before photocopying)
Two players.
Stick the page on to cardboard and cut out. The cards are placed face down and each child takes it in turn to choose two cards.
If the cards match, the child can keep them. If not, he or she puts them back in the same place. The child with the most pairs at the end is the winner.
Alternatively, the cards could be used for a game of 'Snap'.

Money word search

d	l	t	n	p	m	b	i	l	l	r	u	w	l
f	i	g	o	t	e	z	s	c	h	a	n	g	e
d	j	f	y	t	b	n	d	m	x	e	o	v	s
e	r	h	f	k	a	l	c	p	y	m	p	a	s
x	b	u	p	e	v	l	w	e	r	o	m	z	b
c	l	u	a	j	r	h	r	n	d	n	e	c	s
h	d	o	y	k	p	e	i	n	f	e	p	g	p
a	m	t	s	o	c	q	n	y	r	y	r	t	e
n	n	e	c	e	n	i	o	c	s	w	i	u	n
g	f	j	i	l	m	o	b	a	e	y	c	x	t
e	g	p	o	u	n	d	r	x	u	t	e	v	z
h	t	k	p	z	g	n	i	p	p	o	h	s	u
a	d	s	p	e	n	d	s	y	h	i	k	p	v

bill	receipt	exchange	coin	pound
shopping	pence	total	penny	buy
price	change	pay	money	cost
more	less	difference	spend	spent

Teachers' notes (mask before photocopying)
The object is to find the words hidden on the grid and highlight them in some way.
The words on the grid are written horizontally, vertically, diagonally or backwards.

FIRST STEPS – *Using Money Book 3*   © Folens (copiable page)